Carlos Goes Camping

Katie Sharp
Illustrated by Roberta Collier Morales

Harcourt Achieve

Rigby • Saxon • Steck-Vaughn

www.HarcourtAchieve.com
1.800.531.5015

Carlos and Dad are
in a car.

Carlos and Dad are
going camping.

Carlos helps with the tent.
It is fun!

Carlos gets
his sleeping bag.
He puts it
near Dad's
sleeping bag.

"Can you look for sticks?" asked Dad.

"I can look for sticks!" said Carlos.

9

Carlos looks by the tent.

He does not see sticks.

Carlos looks by the car.
He does not see sticks.

Carlos looks in the woods.
He sees sticks!

Dad makes a fire
with the sticks.

Carlos cooks a hot dog.

"I like to camp,"
said Carlos.

"I like to camp, too,"
said Dad.